Richard Rodgers
Choral Collection

The Novello Choral Programme

Novello Publishing Limited
(A division of Music Sales Limited)
8/9 Frith Street, London W1D 3JB, England

Novello

NOV200217
ISBN No. 0-7119-8813-7

Music setting by Stave Origination
Cover design by Michael Bell Design
Cover picture by Katie van Dyck

This edition © 2001 Novello Publishing Limited
Published in Great Britain by Novello Publishing Limited

Head office: 8/9, Frith Street, London W1D 3JB, England

Telephone: +44 (0)20 7434 0066
Fax: +44 (0)20 7287 6329

Sales and hire:
Music Sales Limited,
Newmarket Road, Bury St. Edmunds, Suffolk IP33 3YB

www.musicsales.com

e-mail: music@musicsales.co.uk

All Rights Reserved

Printed in Great Britain

No part of this publication may be copied or
reproduced in any form or by any means without the
prior permission of Novello and Company Limited

The Sorrows of Mary 1

Puer Nobis 9

Lullay mine Liking 14

Spell of Sleep 22

Nowel 32

Full Fathom Five 38

Gloria 49

The Seasons of His Mercies 60

Calico Pie 71

A Contemplation upon Flowers 80

Richard Rodney Bennett was born in Broadstairs, Kent in 1936. He is one of the most versatile of British composer/performers, equally at home writing for the concert hall or for film and as a jazz pianist. He studied at the Royal Academy of Music in London and in Paris, where he became the first pupil of Pierre Boulez. He received the Arnold Bax Society Prize in 1964 and the Ralph Vaughan Williams Award for Composer of the Year in 1965. He was composer-in-residence at the Peabody Institute, Baltimore in 1970–71. As a jazz pianist, singer and composer, Bennett has toured extensively, made several recordings with jazz artists, regularly appearing as a soloist at jazz clubs in New York and elsewhere. In the autumn of 1995 he took up the International Chair of Composition at the Royal Academy of Music.

Bennett's concert works have always been known for their richness of invention and development, elegance and balance. For his inspiration, he has acknowledged such diverse sources as Debussy, Joplin, Monteverdi, the signs of the zodiac, the poetry of Rilke and Herrick, Greek legend, and Kandinsky. His catalogue includes works for a wide variety of forces from solo instrument to full symphony and from brass band to opera. Key works include the opera *The Mines of Sulphur* (1963), Piano Concerto (1968), *Sonnets to Orpheus* (1979), Symphony No. 3 (1987), *Concerto for Stan Getz* (1990) and *Partita* (1995).

Recent commissions have included *Reflections on a 16th Century Tune*, *Rondel for large jazz ensemble* premiered by the London Sinfonietta (1999) as tribute to Duke Ellington, the incidental music to the BBC drama *Gormenghast* (1999) and *The Glory and the Dream* (2000) a setting of Wordsworth for choir and organ for the New Cambridge Singers and a consortium of fifteen other choirs from around the world.

In 1977 Richard Rodney Bennett was appointed CBE and in 1998 he received a knighthood for services to music. He lives in New York.

The Sorrows of Mary

Text:
15th century anonymous

RICHARD RODNEY BENNETT

Music published by arrangement with Universal Edition (London) Ltd.

© 1965 Oxford University Press. Reproduced by permission.

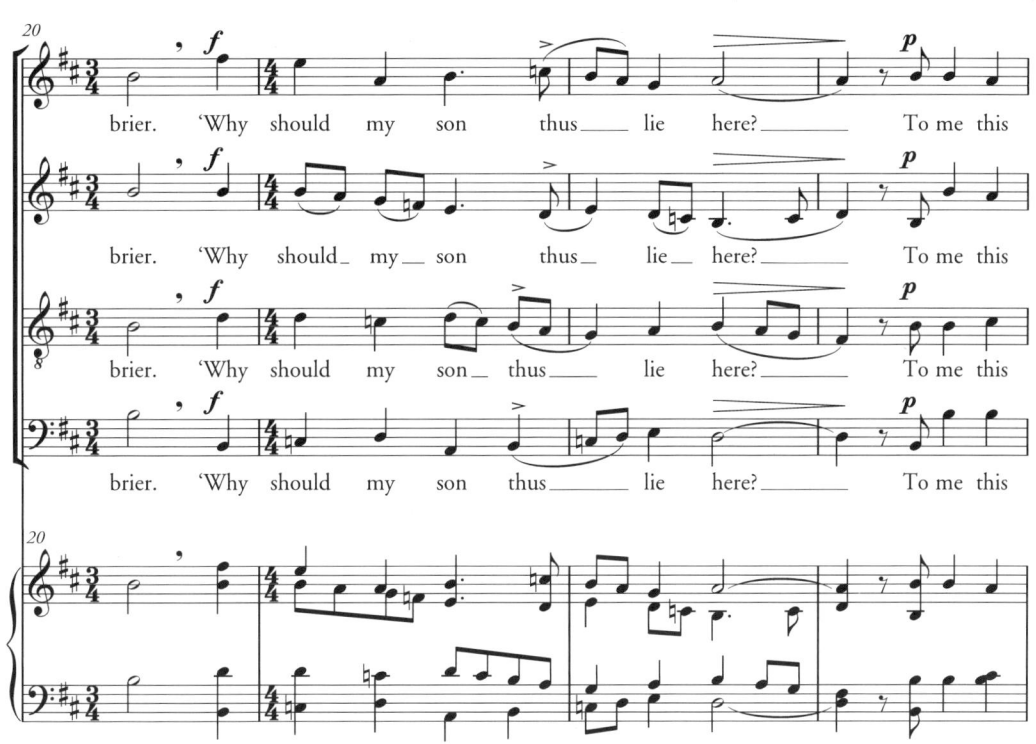

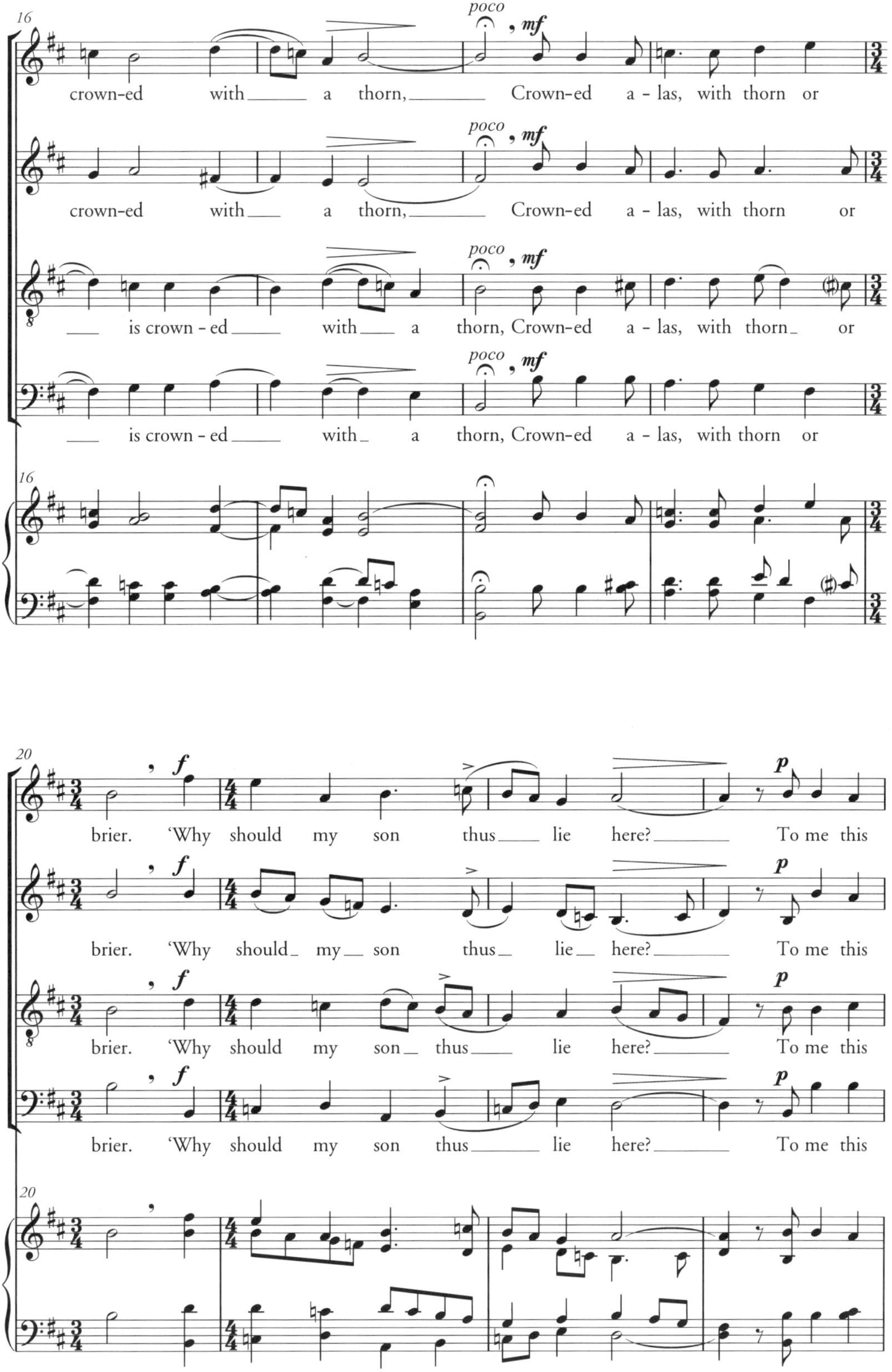
16
poco
mf
crown-ed with a thorn, Crown-ed a - las, with thorn or
is crown - ed with a thorn, Crown-ed a - las, with thorn or
16
20
f
brier. 'Why should my son thus lie here?
p
To me this
20

To the Marchioness of Aberdeen

Puer Nobis

Text:
Alice Meynell

RICHARD RODNEY BENNETT

© Copyright 1983 Novello & Company Limited

long. Ev'n as the cold keen win-ter grows not old, As
long. Ev'n as the cold keen win-ter grows not old, As
long. Ev'n as the cold keen win-ter grows not old, As
long. Ev'n as the cold keen win-ter grows not old, As

child-hood is so fresh, fore-seen, And spring in the fa-
child-hood is so fresh, fore-seen, And spring in the fa-
child-hood is so fresh, fore-seen, And spring in the fa-
child-hood is so fresh, fore-seen, And spring in the fa-

21
poco dim.
p
cresc.
-mi - liar green. Sud - den as sweet Come the ex -
24
f
p subito
-pect - ed feet, All joy is young and new all art, And

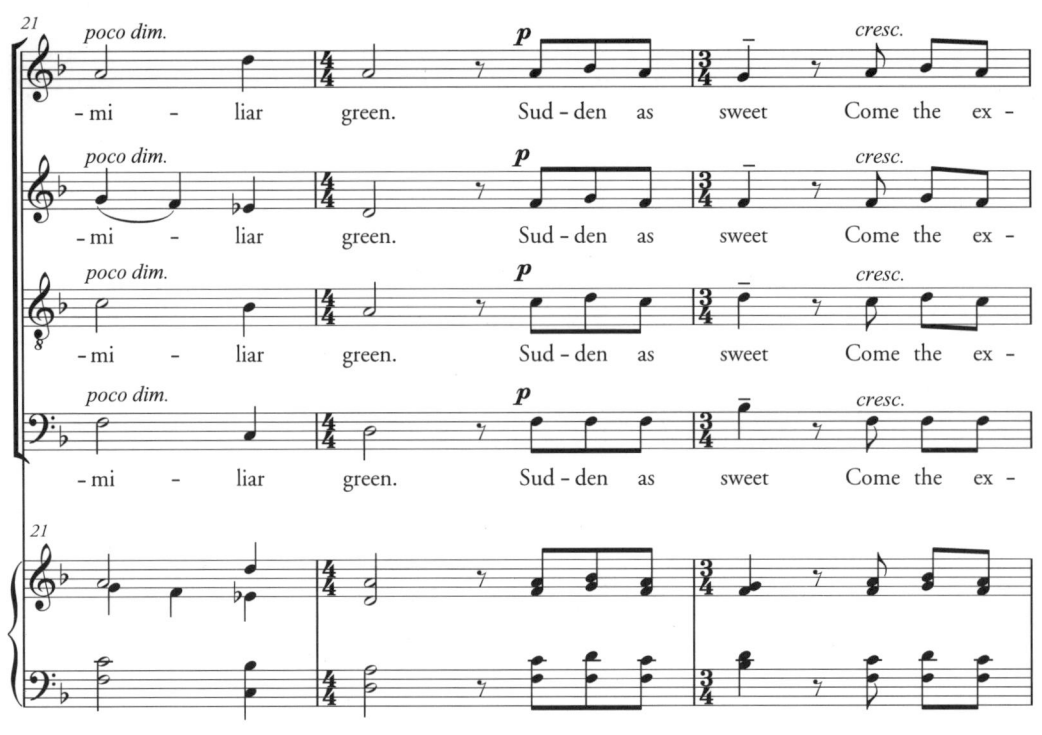

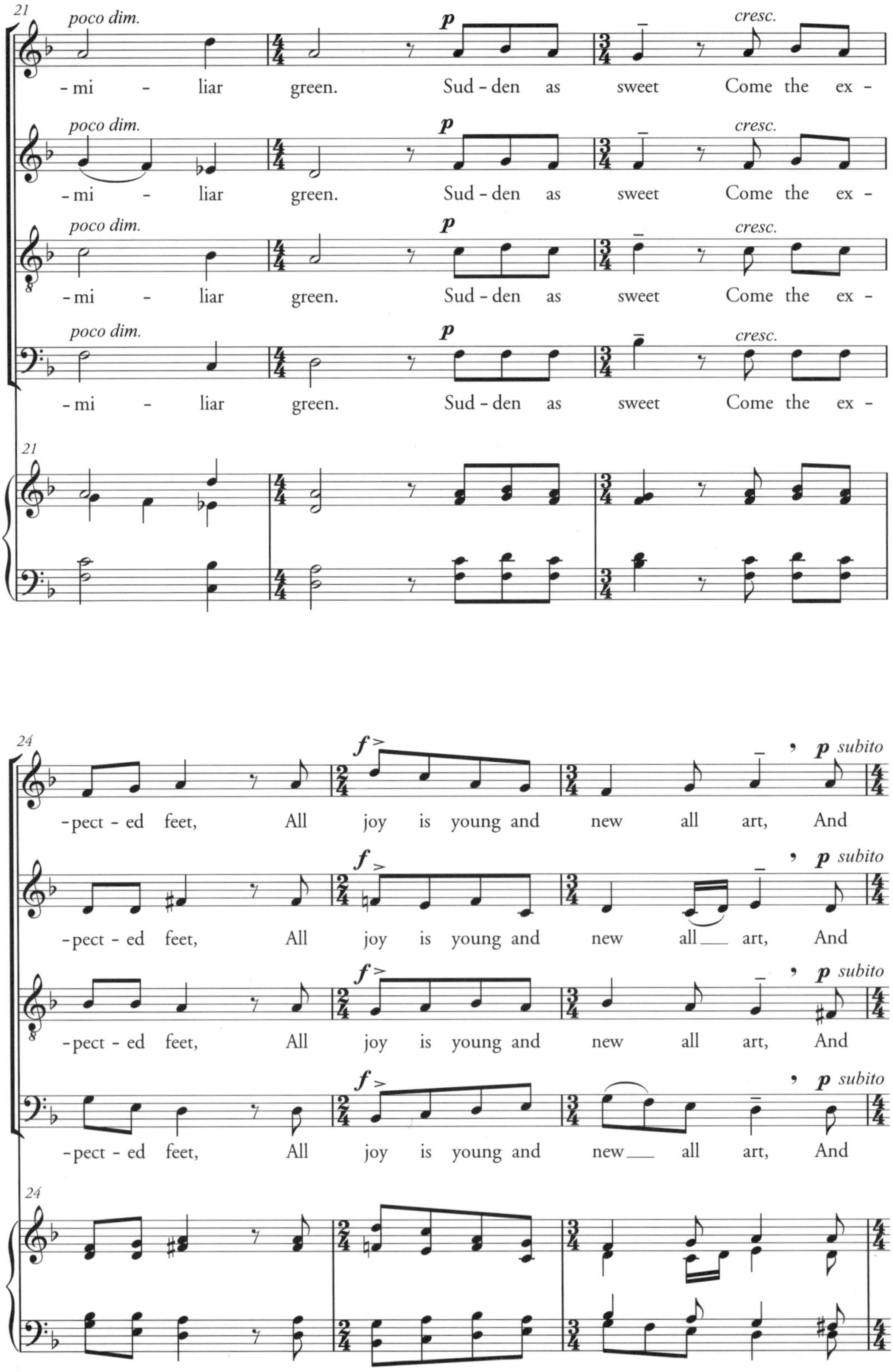

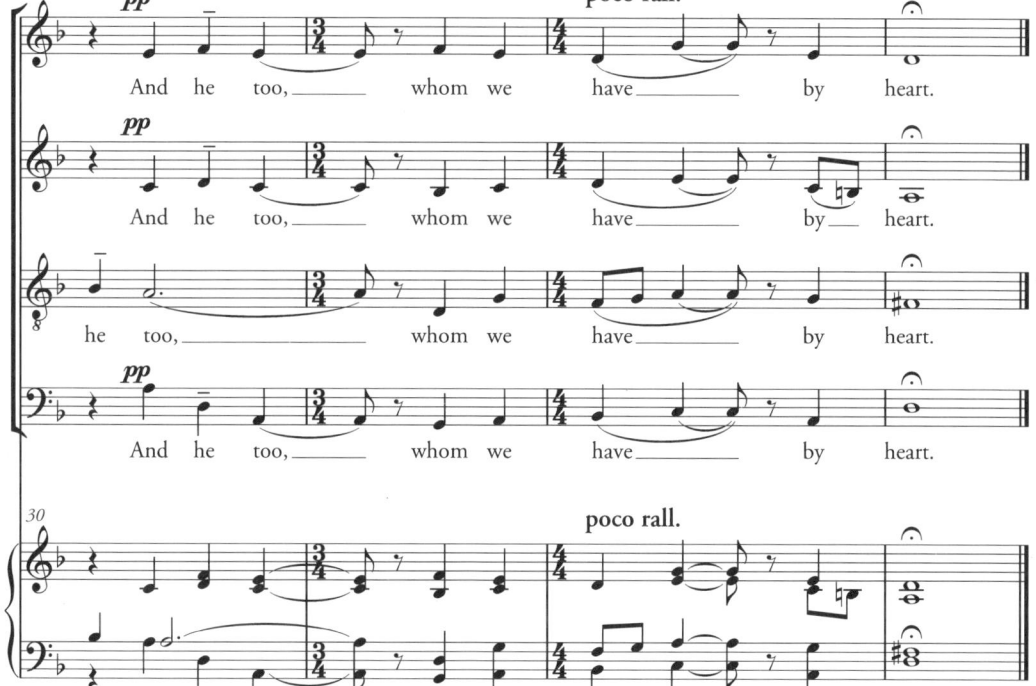

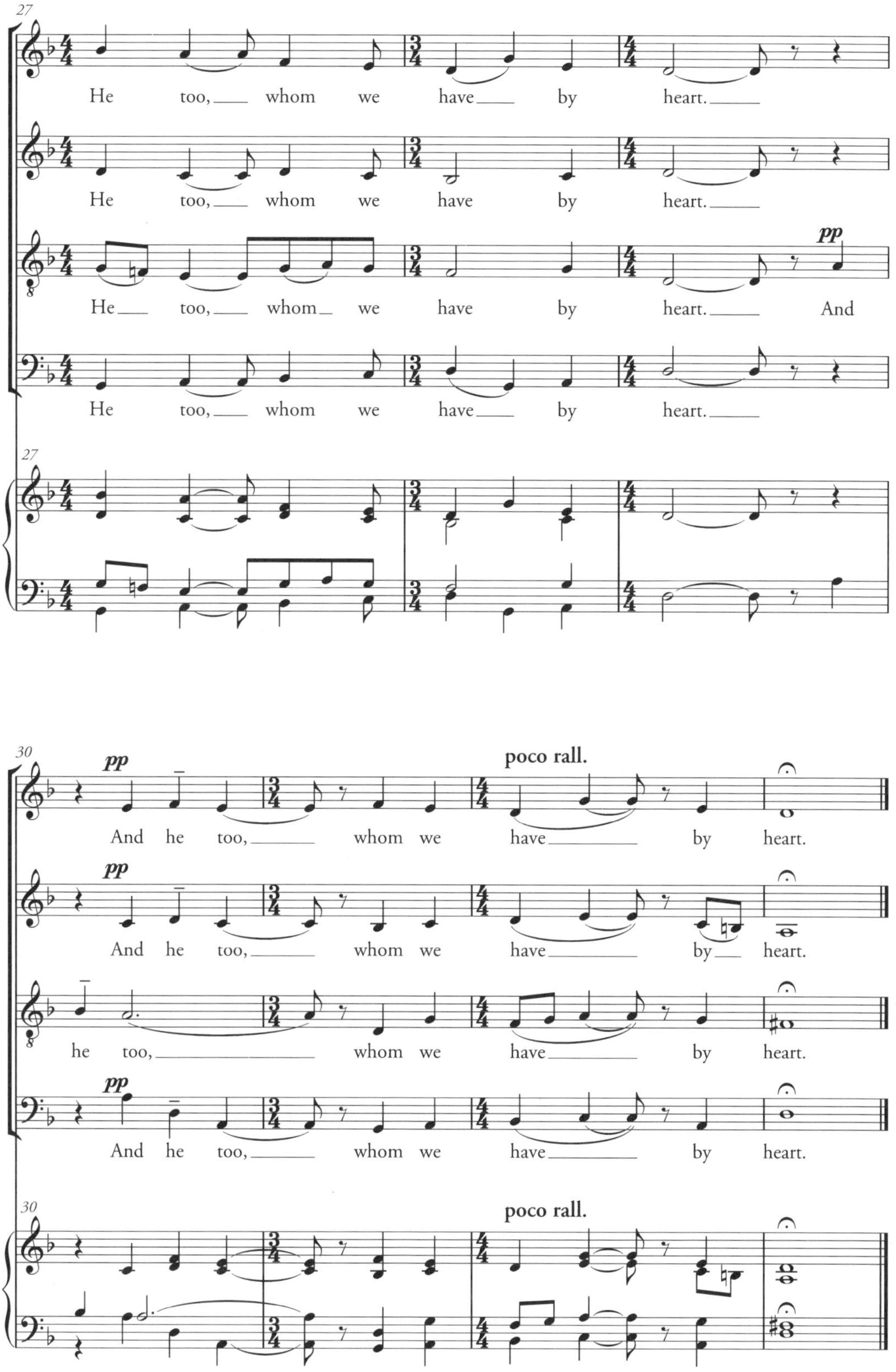
27
He too, whom we have by heart.
He too, whom we have by heart.
pp
He too, whom we have by heart. And
He too, whom we have by heart.
27
30
pp
poco rall.
And he too, whom we have by heart.
pp
And he too, whom we have by heart.
he too, whom we have by heart.
pp
And he too, whom we have by heart.
30
poco rall.

14

for the Rt. Hon. Edward Heath

Lullay mine Liking

Text:
Anon

RICHARD RODNEY BENNETT

© Copyright 1985 Novello & Company Limited

14
(Tutti)
mp
lit - tle Child, A sweee - te Lord - ing. Lul - lay mine Lik - ing, my dear Son, my
Lul - lay mine Lik - ing, my dear Son, my
Lul - lay my Son, my
Lul - lay my Son, my
20
mf
Sweet - ing; Lul - lay my dear Heart, mine own dear Dar - ling.
(Solo opt.)
mp
Sweet - ing; Lul - lay mine own dear Dar - ling. That E - ter - nal
Sweet - ing Lul - lay my dear Heart, mine own dear Dar - ling.
Sweet - ing; Lul - lay my Dar - ling.

22

to Jane Manning and the choirs of the Three Choirs Festival

Spell of Sleep

Text:
Kathleen Raine

RICHARD RODNEY BENNETT

Poem taken from the *Collected Poems of Kathleen Raine*, by kind permission of Messrs. Hamish Hamilton.
Spell of Sleep forms the fourth movement of *Spells* for soprano solo, mixed chorus and orchestra.
Available from the publisher, order no. NOV072307

© 1986 Novello & Company Limited

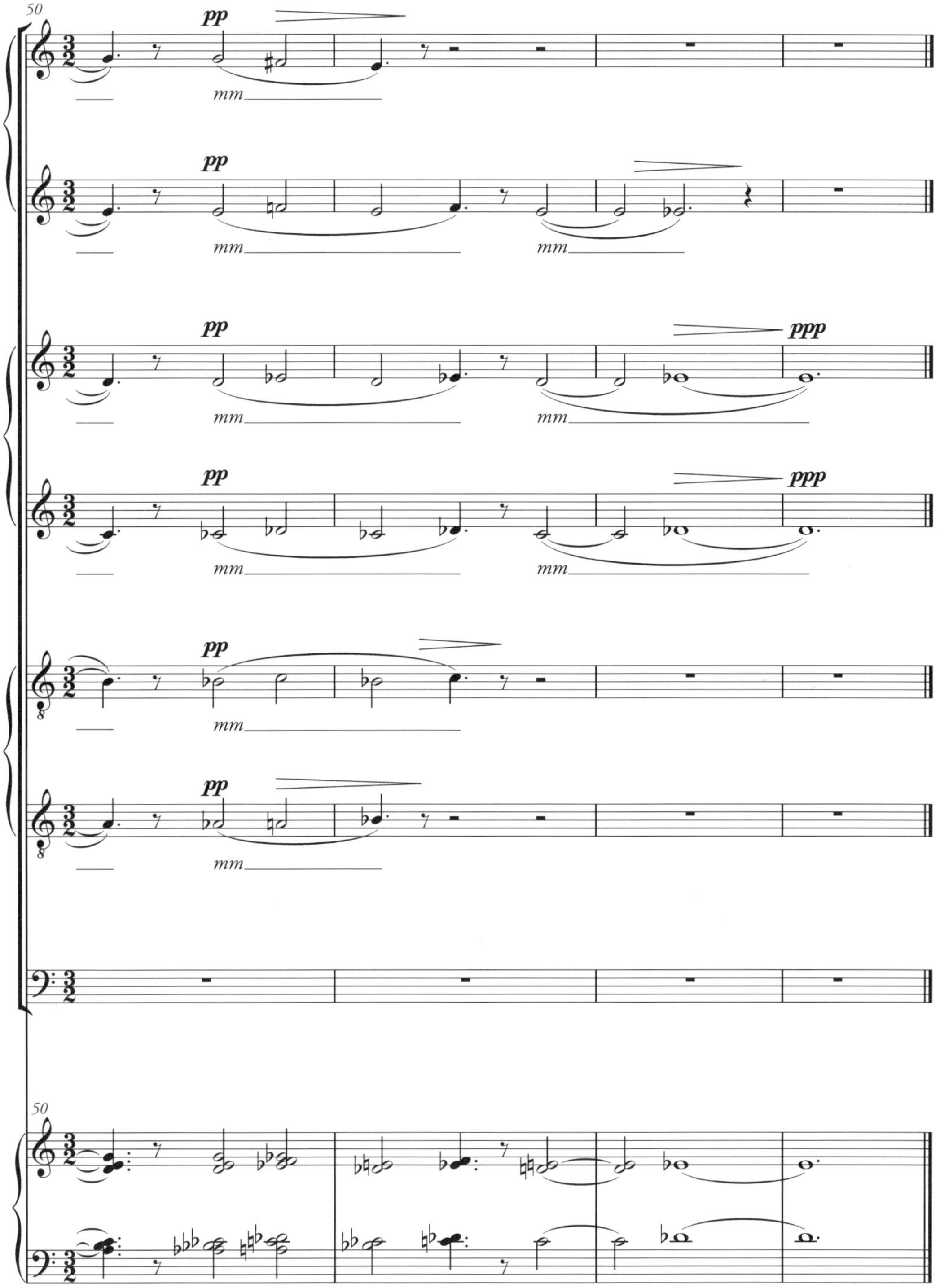
50
pp
mm
pp
mm
mm
pp
ppp
mm
mm
pp
ppp
mm
mm
pp
mm
pp
mm
50

for the choir of King's College, Cambridge

Nowel

Text:
Walter de la Mare

RICHARD RODNEY BENNETT

© 1987 Novello & Company Limited

Text by Walter de la Mare reproduced by permission of The Literary Trustees of Walter de la Mare and The Society of Authors as their representative.

10
Christ - mas eve is come, and lo, Wild clash the bells a -
No-wel, no-wel, No-wel, no - wel, No-wel, no-wel, No-wel, no-
Christ - mas eve is come, and lo, Wild clash the bells a -
No-wel, no-wel, No-wel, no - wel, No-wel, no-wel, No-wel, no-
10
15
(f sempre)
- cross the snow, Waits in the dark streets ca - rol - ling go;
- wel, No - wel, no - wel, No - wel, no - wel,
(f sempre)
- cross the snow, Waits in the dark streets ca - rol - ling go;
(f sempre)
- wel, No - wel, no - wel, No - wel, no - wel,
15

19
ff appassionato
‘No - wel! No-wel!’ they shout and oh, How
No - wel, no - wel, No - wel, no-wel, oh, How
No - wel, no - wel, No - wel, no-wel, oh, How
24
f
mp espressivo
live out the day! Each breath I breathe turns
mp
live out the day! No - wel, no - wel No-wel, no-

35

38
mf
The can - dles daz - zle in my eyes, And
mf
dream; No - wel, no - wel, No - wel, no - wel, No - wel,
mf
dream; No - wel, no - wel, No - wel, no - wel, No - wel,
mf
The can - dles daz - zle in my eyes, And
38
42
cresc.
ev - 'ry leap - ing fire - flame tries To sing what none could say.
cresc.
no - wel, No - wel, no - wel, No - wel, no - wel, No-
cresc.
no - wel, No - wel, no - wel, No - wel, no - wel, No-
cresc.
ev - 'ry leap - ing fire - flame tries To sing what none could say.
42

37

38

for Donald Hunt

Full fathom five

Text:
Shakespeare: The Tempest

RICHARD RODNEY BENNETT

A minimum of 24 singers is required.
Tubular bell should be placed out of sight of the audience.

Full fathom five is taken from *Sea Change* for unaccompanied choir.
Available from the publisher, order no. NOV070490

© Copyright 1989 Novello & Company Limited

4
mp
Of his bones are co - rall, are
mp
Of his bones are co - rall, are
(p)
Of his bones are co-rall made, Of his bones
mp
Of his bones are co - rall, are
p
lies, Of his bones are co - rall made,
mp
Fa - ther lies, Of his bones are co - rall,
mp
lies, Of his bones are co - rall,
mp
lies, Of his bones are co - rall,

40

10
dim.
p
that were his eyes, his eyes, No -
dim.
p
that were his eyes, his eyes, No -
dim.
p
that were his eyes, his eyes, No -
dim.
p
those are pearles that were his eyes, his eyes,
dim.
ossia
p
pearles that were his eyes, his eyes,
dim.
were his eyes, those are pearles that were his eyes,
dim.
p
pearles that were his eyes, his eyes,
dim.
p
pearles that were his eyes, his eyes,

13
cresc. poco a poco
- thing of him, no - thing of him that doth
cresc. poco a poco
- thing of him, no - thing of him that doth
cresc. poco a poco
- thing of him, no - thing of him that doth
cresc. poco a poco
No - thing of him, of him that doth fade,
cresc. poco a poco
No - thing of him, no - thing of him
cresc. poco a poco
No - thing of him, of him that doth fade, that
cresc. poco a poco
No - thing of him, no - thing of him
cresc. poco a poco
No - thing of him, no - thing of him

16
f ma dolce
fade, But doth suf - fer a sea - change
fade, But doth suf - fer a sea - change
fade, But doth suf - fer a sea - change
that doth fade, But doth suf - fer a sea - change
that doth fade, But doth suf - fer a sea - change
doth fade, But doth suf - fer a sea - change
that doth fade, But doth suf - fer a sea - change
that doth fade, But doth suf - fer a sea - change

44

23
p dolciss.
Sea - Nimphs hour - ly ring his Knell.
p dolciss.
Sea - Nimphs hour - ly ring his Knell.
p dolciss.
ossia
Sea - Nimphs hour - ly ring his
p
p
ding, ding, ding,
p dolciss.
Sea - Nimphs hour - ly ring his
p
dong. dong.
p dolciss.
Sea - Nimphs hour - ly ring his knell.
p dolciss.
Sea - Nimphs hour - ly ring his knell.

46

47

34
dim. a niente
-dong, ding - - dong.
dim. a niente
-dong, ding - - dong.
dim. a niente
ding - dong, ding - dong.
ding.
ding - dong, ding - dong.
dong.
ding - dong.

Gloria

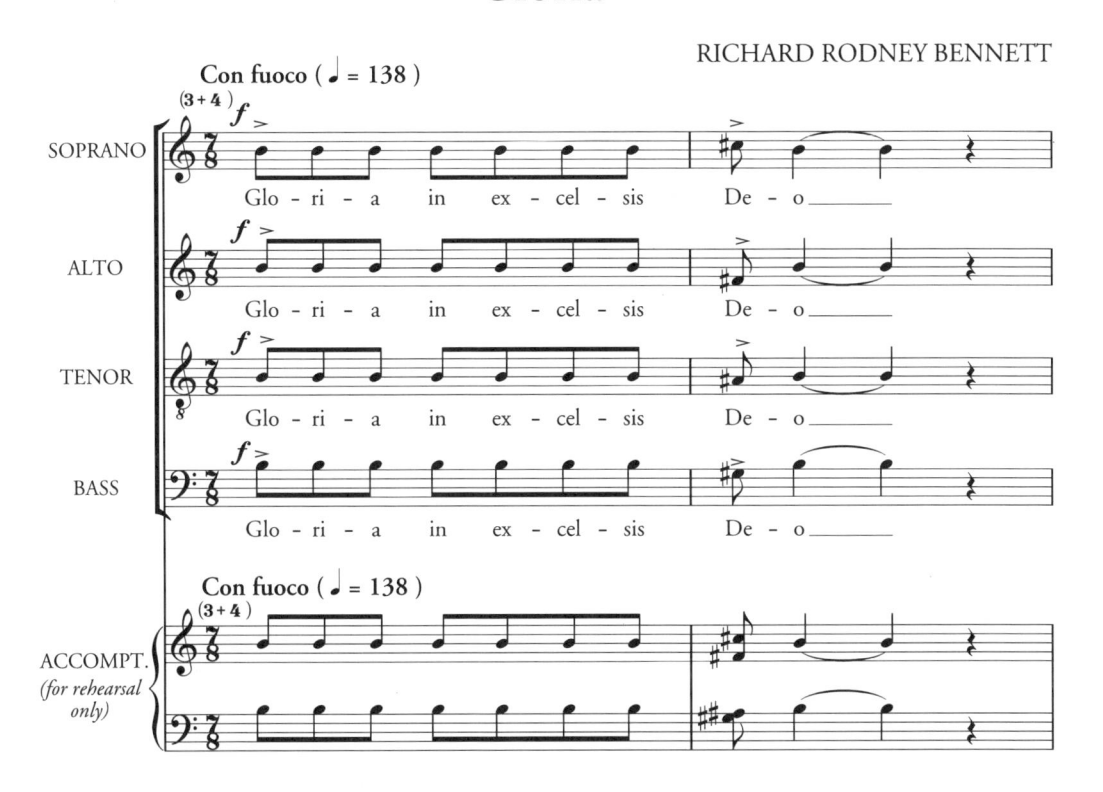

RICHARD RODNEY BENNETT

© Copyright 1990 Novello & Company Limited

Gloria forms the second movement of *Missa Brevis* for chorus a capella. Available from the publisher, order no. NOV290711

sempre
(2+3+2)
p ritmico
- mi - ni - bus bo - nae vo - lun - ta - tis Lau - da - mus te
ritmico
(3+4)
Be - ne - di - ci - mus te A - do - ra - mus te Glo - ri - fi - ca - mus te

13
(p) cresc. poco a poco
Gra - ti - as a - gi - mus ti - bi prop - ter mag-nam
17
(3+4)
f
glo - ri - am tu - am Do-mi-ne De-us Rex coe-les - tis

21
(3+4) mf
De - us Pa - ter om - ni - po - tens Do - mi - ne Fi - li
mf
(3+4)
24
poco rit.
p
u - ni - ge - ni - te Je - su Chri - ste
poco rit.

a tempo, sempre mosso (𝅗𝅥 = 69)
29
p semplice
poco cresc.
Do - mi-ne De - us, Ag - nus De - i Fi - li-us
Do - mi - ne De - us Ag - nus De - i Fi - li-
a tempo, sempre mosso (𝅗𝅥 = 69)
34
mf
Pa - tris Qui tol-lis pec-ca-ta mun - di Mi - se-re-re
Mi-se-re - re
-us Pa - tris Qui tol-lis pec-ca-ta mun - di Mi - se -
-us Pa - tris Qui tol-lis pec-ca-ta mun-di Mi - se -

38
mp
no - bis Qui tol - lis pec - ca - ta mun - di su - sci - pe de - pre-
mp
no - bis Qui tol - lis pec - ca - ta mun - di su - sci - pe de - pre-
mp
- re - re Qui tol - lis pec - ca - ta mun - di su - sci - pe de - pre-
mp
- re - re Qui tol - lis pec - ca - ta mun - di su - sci - pe de - pre-
f
38
42
mf
- ca - ti - o - nem nos - tram Qui se - des ad dex - te - ram
- ca - ti - o - nem nos - tram Qui se - des ad dex - te - ram
- ca - ti - o - nem nos - tram Qui se - des ad dex - te - ram
- ca - ti - o - nem nos - tram Qui se - des ad dex - te - ram

46
ff
f
ff
Pa - tris Mi - se - re - re no - bis Mi - se - re - re
Pa - tris Mi - se - re - re no - bis Mi - se - re - re
Pa - tris Mi - se - re - re no - bis Mi - se - re - re
Pa - tris Mi - se - re - re no - bis Mi - se - re - re
46

50
f
mf
dim.
poco rit.
no - bis Mi - se - re - re no - bis no - bis
no - bis Mi - se - re - re no - bis no - bis
no - bis Mi - se - re - re no - bis no - bis
no - bis Mi - se - re - re no - bis no - bis
50
poco rit.

55
Come prima
(p)
(3+2)
f
Quo-ni-am tu so-lus san-ctus tu so-lus
Quo-ni-am tu so-lus san-ctus tu so-lus
Quo-ni-am tu so-lus san-ctus tu so-lus
Quo-ni-am tu so-lus san-ctus tu so-lus
55
(3+2) Come prima

60
(3+2)
ff
f
do-mi-nus tu so-lus al-tis-si-mus Je-su
do-mi-nus tu so-lus al-tis-si-mus Je-su
do-mi-nus tu so-lus al-tis-si-mus Je-su
do-mi-nus tu so-lus al-tis-si-mus Je-su
60
(3+2)

57

70
a tempo
p
cresc. poco a poco
Cum sanc - to spi - ri - tu in glo -
70
a tempo
75
f
(3+4)
- - ri - a De - i Pa - tris Cum sanc-to spi - ri - tu in
75
(3+4)

glo - ri - a Cum sanc - to spi - ri - tu in glo - ri - a De - i

Pa - tris A - - - - - - men.

60

to the King's Singers
The Seasons of His Mercies

Text:
John Donne

RICHARD RODNEY BENNETT

The Seasons of His Mercies is taken from *Sermons and Devotions* for six male voices.
Available from the publisher, order no. NOV360060

© Copyright 1992 Novello & Company Limited

earth but in their sea-sons; But God hath made no de-cree to dis-tin-guish the sea-sons of his mer-cies;

12
pp dolciss.
p
In Pa - ra - dise the fruits were ripe the first min - ute, and in
In Pa - ra - dise the fruits were ripe the first min - ute, and in
In Pa - ra - dise the fruits were ripe the first
In Pa - ra - dise the fruits were ripe the first min - ute, and in hea -
In Pa - ra - dise the fruits were ripe the first min - ute and in hea -
15
mp
hea - ven it is al - ways Au - tumne,
hea - ven it is al - ways Au - tumne,
- ven it is al - ways Au - tumne,
- ven it is al - ways Au - tumne,

pochiss. rit.
his mer - cies are ev - er in their ma - tu - ri - ty.
his mer - cies are ev - er in their ma - tu - ri - ty.
his mer - cies are ev - er in their ma - tu - ri - ty.
his mer - cies are ev - er in their ma - tu - ri - ty.
pochiss. rit.
Poco più mosso, liberamente (♩ = ca 66)
TENOR
mf declamento
If some King of the earth have so large an ex - tent of do - mi - ni - on,
in North, and South, as that he hath Win - ter and Sum - mer to - geth - er
in his Do - mi - ni - ons, so large an ex - tent East and West as that he hath
day and night to - geth - er in his Do - mi - ni - ons, much more hath God
mer - cy and judge - ment to - geth - - - - er.
molto f
breve

come prima (♩ = 60)
He brought light out of dark - nesse, not out of a les - ser light; he can
bring thy sum - mer out of win - ter, though thou have no spring;

65

clouded and eclypsed, damped and benummed, smothered and stupefied till now, till now, now

35
God comes to thee, Not as in the dawn-ing of the
God comes to thee, Not as in the dawn-ing of the
God comes to thee, Not as in the dawn-ing
God comes to thee, Not as in the dawn-ing
35
37
day, not as in the bud of the spring, but as the
day, not as in the bud of the spring, but as the
of the day, as in the bud of the spring, but as the
of the day, as in the bud of the spring, but as the
37

sun____ at noon____ to il - lus -
sun____ at noon____ to il - lus -
sun____ at____ noon_____ to
sun____ at____ noon_____ to

- trate all shad - owes,_____ as____ the sheaves____
- trate all shad - owes,_____ as____ the sheaves____
il - lus - trate all shad - owes,_____ as____ the
il - lus - trate all shad - owes,_____ as____ the

in har-vest, to fill all
in har-vest, to fill all
sheaves in har-vest, to fill all
sheaves in har-vest, to fill all

pochiss. rit. **a tempo, sostenuto**

pe-nu-ries,

pe-nu-ries, all oc-ca-sions in-vite his

pe-nu-ries,

pe-nu-ries,

49
pp
and all times, and all times, and
mer - cies, and all times, and all times, and
and all times, all times,
and all times, all times,
52
poco rit.
mp
p
pp
all times are his sea - sons.
all times are his sea - sons.
all times are his sea - sons.
all times are his sea - sons.

for Stephen Wilkinson

Calico Pie

Text:
Edward Lear

RICHARD RODNEY BENNETT

© Copyright 1998 Novello & Company Limited

Calico Pie is taken from *Calico Pie:* five poems of Edward Lear for chorus a cappella.
Available from the publisher, order no. NOV160256

9
mf
Till a - way they flew,
sang Till a - way they flew, And they
f sub.
sang Till a - way they flew,
Till a - way they flew, And they
13
f
mf
They ne-ver came back, they ne-ver came back, ne-ver came back, ne-ver came
ne-ver came back to me! ne-ver came back, ne-ver came back, ne-ver came
dim.
They ne-ver came back, they ne-ver came back, ne-ver came back, ne-ver came
ne-ver came back to me! ne-ver came back, ne-ver came back, ne-ver came

17
p
mp
back to me! Cal - li - co Jam, The lit - tle Fish
back to me! Ca - li - co Jam, The
back to me! Ca - li - co Jam, The
back to me! Ca - li - co Jam, The
22
p
cresc.
swam, o - ver the syl - la - bub sea, He took off his hat
lit - tle Fish swam, He took off his

26
f
To the Sole and the Sprat, and the Wil - le - by - wat, But he
hat To the Sole and the Sprat,
f
hat To the Sole and the Sprat, But he
(♭)
hat To the Sole and the Sprat,
26

30
mf
dim.
ne-ver came back to me! ne-ver came back, ne-ver came back, ne-ver came
f
mf
dim.
He ne-ver came back, he ne-ver came back, ne-ver came back, ne-ver came
mf
dim.
ne-ver came back to me! ne-ver came back, ne-ver came back, ne-ver came
f
mf
dim.
He ne-ver came back, he ne-ver came back, ne-ver came back, ne-ver came
30

34
p
mp leggiero
back to me! -li - co the
p
mp marc.
back to me! Ca - li - co Ban The lit - tle mice
p
mp leggiero
back to me! -li - co the
p
mp
back to me! Ca - li - co Ban, The
34
39
mice To be rea - dy for tea,
ran To be rea - dy in time for tea,
mice To be rea - dy for tea,
lit - tle mice ran To be rea - dy for tea,
39

43
(mp)
cresc.
Flip - pe - ty flup, They drank it all up, And danced in the
Flip - pe - ty flup, They drank it all up, And danced in the cup
Flip - pe - ty flup, They drank it all up, And danced in the
Flip - pe - ty flup, They drank it all up And danced in the
43

47
f
mf
meno marc.
cup, But they ne - ver came back to me! They
But they ne - ver ne - ver came back to me! They
cup, But they ne - ver, ne - ver came back to me! They
cup, But they ne - ver, ne - ver came back They
47

ne - ver, ne - ver, ne - ver came back to me!

ne - ver, ne - ver, ne - ver came back to me!

ne - ver, ne - ver, ne - ver came back to me!

ne - ver, ne - ver, ne - ver came back to me!

Ca - li - co Drum, The Grass hop - pers come, The But - ter - fly,

Ca - li - co Drum, The Grass hop - pers come, The But - ter - fly,

Ca - li - co Drum, The Grass hop - pers come, The But - ter - fly,

Ca - li - co Drum, The Grass hop - pers come, The But - ter - fly,

Bee-tle and Bee,____ o - ver the ground, A - round and round____
Bee-tle and Bee,____ o - ver the ground,____ A - round and round____
Bee-tle and Bee,____ o - ver the ground, A - round____ and
Bee-tle and Bee,____ o - ver the ground, A - round____ and

____with a hop and a bound,____ But they ne - ver came back to
____with a hop and a bound,____ But they ne - ver came back to
round, with a hop and a bound,____ But they ne - ver came back to
round, with a hop and a bound,____ But they ne - ver came back to

me! They never came back, never came back, they
me! They never came back, never came back, they
me! They never came back, ne - ver came back,
me! They never came back, ne - ver came back,

never came back, never came back, they never came back to me!
never came back, never came back, they never came back to me!
never came back, never came back, they never came back to me!
never came back, never came back, they never came back to me!

*for Philip Barnes and the St Louis Chamber Chorus
and in memory of John Philips*

A Contemplation upon Flowers

Text:
Henry King (b.1592)

RICHARD RODNEY BENNETT

© Copyright 1999 Novello & Company Limited

harm-less show, And to your beds of earth a-gain; you are not
harm - less show, And to your beds of earth a-gain; you are not
harm - less show, And to your beds of earth a-gain;
harm - less show, And to your beds of earth a-gain;

proud you know your birth, For your em-broi-dered gar-ments are from
proud you know your birth, For your em-broi-dered gar-ments are from
you are not proud, you know your birth, For your em-broi-dered gar-ments
you are not proud, you know your birth, For your em-broi-dered gar-ments

earth. You do o-bey your months and times but I would have it,
earth. You do o-bey your months and times but I would have it,
are from earth. You do o-bey your months and times but I would
are from earth. You do o-bey your months and times but I would

would have it ev - er Spring, ev - er spring, ev - er
would have it ev - er Spring, ev - er spring, ev - er
have it ev - er Spring, ev - er spring, ev - er
have it ev - er Spring, ev - er spring, ev - er

spring. My fate would know no winter, never die Nor think of such a thing, Oh, that I

25
could my bed of earth but view And smile and look as cheer - ful - ly as
could my bed of earth but view And smile and look as cheer - ful - ly as
could my bed of earth but view And smile and look as
could my bed of earth but view And smile and look as
25
tenuto - - - - - - con moto
28
f appass.
mf
you. Oh teach me, teach me to see death, and
you. Oh teach me to see death and not
you. Oh teach me to see death and not
you. Oh teach me to see death and not
tenuto - - - - - - con moto
28

not to fear / But ra-ther to take truce;
to fear / But ra-ther to take truce;
to fear / But ra-ther to take truce;
to fear / But ra-ther to take truce;

How of-ten have I seen you at a bier, And
How of-ten have I seen you at a bier,
How of-ten have I seen you at a bier,
How of-ten have I seen you at a bier,

there look fresh and spruce; you fra - grant flow-ers,

And there look fresh and spruce; you fra - grant flow-ers,

And there look fresh and spruce; you fra - grant flow-ers,

And there look fresh and spruce; you fra - grant flow-ers,

then teach me, teach me that my breath like yours may

then teach me, teach me that my breath like yours may

teach me, then teach me that my breath like yours may

teach me, then teach me that my breath like yours may

87